Sketches of Athens

Twelve Character Piano Pieces with Poems

by Liguang Zhou

Dorrance Publishing Co
585 Alpha Drive
Suite 103
Pittsburgh, PA 15238
Visit our website at *www.dorrancebookstore.com*

ISBN: 978-1-6480-4576-9
eISBN: 978-1-6480-4662-9

Sketches of Athens

Twelve Character Piano Pieces with Poems

Dedicated to Ohio University Professor of Piano, Dr. Christopher Fisher

Acknowledgment

First, I want to express gratitude to Dr. Christopher Fisher for his teaching and guidance during my master's degree at the Ohio University School of Music. I also want to thank Dr. Richard Wetzel, who is chair of graduate studies at the OU School of Music. He provided his encouragement and support for me to write this work. Moreover, I want to send my special thanks to Dr. Mark Phillips, who is professor emeritus in composition at Ohio University. I appreciate his time and willingness to share his thoughts and ideas about this work.

In addition, I feel thankful for the help of Matthew Dowler, who is a composition major at the Ohio University School of Music. He spent valuable time helping me solve technical issues of the Sebelius software. I must express my gratefulness to my dear friend, Dr. Behzad Namazi, composer and fellow OU alumnus, for his enthusiastic review and revision of my compositions.

Further, I appreciate the help from Dr. Ronald Green and Louisa Green, who have been generous in offering their time to help me edit and revise these notes and poems.

Table of Contents

Notes

I studied at the Ohio University School of Music from August of 2013 to May of 2015, pursuing my master's degree in piano performance. Before I came to the United States to study, I lived in Shenyang, China. My experiences were a little unusual. I did not travel in China, and I did not even travel very much in my hometown. I knew only a few places—school and three bookstores. I usually just stayed home for practicing and composing. So, I really did not know very much about my hometown, China, or the world.

After I graduated from Shenyang Conservatory of Music, I was determined to go to the United States to study. Through my former teacher, Dr. Tianshu Wang's introduction, I contacted Dr. Christopher Fisher, piano professor and chair of the piano department at the Ohio University School of Music. He and I kept in touch for three years before I came to OU to study with him.

Athens, Ohio, was like my second hometown. I felt I lived in a new world. I found myself really enjoying Ohio University and the town of Athens. Under Dr. Fisher's guidance my music career really started there, where I performed solo recitals, chamber music, and concerts with the Wind Symphony, the University Singers, and the Symphony Orchestra. After I graduated from OU, I studied and then obtained my DMA in piano performance at The Ohio State University School of Music in Columbus, Ohio, which is not far from Athens. I have often had opportunities to revisit Athens.

During my educations at OU and OSU, I traveled widely in the United States and became convinced that Athens and Ohio University were special: People are kind and enthusiastic, professors are patient and conscientious, and friends are welcoming and supportive. That is what motivates this work. *Sketches of Athens* expresses my genuine love of Ohio University and Athens, Ohio. In this set of piano works, I have portrayed twelve different themes from my relationship with Athens, themes drawn from common events in Athens and from some of my own experiences. For me, they were all important and unforgettable.

Two influences led me to compose this work. The first is that of my piano professor, Dr. Christopher Fisher, who is a dedicated pedagogue and a wonderful pianist; his books about piano teaching and the music he composed for his students are an inspiration for this work. For instance, *Teaching Piano in Groups* (book) and *Sunrise over the Yangtze* (piano music) are excellent resources for teaching piano. Another resource came from browsing some other piano music for piano pedagogy. Many Ohio piano teachers, such as William Gillock, composed pedagogical pieces for their students. Following such examples, I also wanted to compose music for my students to study and perform.

Three Elements in
Sketches of Athens

1. Eclecticism

Current pedagogical pieces are focused primarily on reading and basic piano techniques as the foundation of piano playing. In my short lyrical piano pieces, I wanted to follow this tradition, as well. Also, I wanted to train students regarding musicality and aesthetics. In the twenty-first century, we are exposed to many different styles in art music. Not only can we study the music of Baroque, Classical, and Romantic styles, but we can move forward to experience a variety of musical styles and even combine styles in individual pieces. As my experiment, this set of twelve pieces is eclectic and poly-stylistic.

2. Quotations from Beethoven

I have no desire to lose the European music tradition in my compositions. Thus, for each individual piece, I included a musical quotation from Beethoven. These quoted melodies are all iconic, such as For Elise and Ode to Joy. It will not be difficult to find the Beethoven quotations in the pieces. The value of classicism is that it is the root of art music. My purpose is to trigger interest and curiosity about classical repertoire within the eclecticism.

3. Poems

I wrote twelve poems to invite the students to interpret the music. Poetry and music were closely connected in ancient Greece. Over music history, many great composers, such as Beethoven, Liszt, Robert Schumann, and Rachmaninoff, were inspired by literatures. A great number of their works were influenced by poems and novels. For these masters, music was not just a type of art, but more like a vehicle to express complex emotions. In this set of twelve piano pieces, each individual piece of music can be paired with a poem. Now, a common issue in piano playing and teaching is that students just focus on the musical notes, instead of feeling the music in their souls. They should pour their emotions intothe music. I think poetry can be helpful for piano students to open their imaginations and guide them to interpreting music from their hearts.

Sketches of Athens
（雅典素描）

1. The Unforgettable Energy of Spring
2. The Nighttime in Athens
3. Dr. Fisher's Studio Party
4. Summertime in Athens
5. Busy Court Street
6. Ohio University, the Beautiful
7. Beautiful October
8. OU Boys and Girls
9. Halloween Party in Athens
10. Christmas Eve in Athens
11. Christmas Day in Athens
12. Going Back to Ohio University

1. The Unforgettable Energy of Spring

Spring is walking towards the small town quietly.
You could not know it is coming towards us strongly.
We sense that not by our eyes and ears, but by our hearts.

We are awaiting the warmer temperature, and the beautiful weather.
And we are longing for a fruitful Spring Semester.
Why are we so sensitive to this?
We are immersed in the graceful season, and we are full of energy, passion, and love.
But we forgot to ask why.

It is probably the first warmer breeze from Appalachian Mountains.
It is probably from the forests turning green.
It is also probably from the atmosphere in Athens: sunny, rainy, and windy.
It is most likely from all the facts that bring us the acuteness of curiosity and hope.

2. The Nighttime in Athens

Night in Athens is tranquil.
You still hear the birds' chirpings.
Those made me know what happiness is—
Sky in dark blue,
Bright stars,
The shape of mountains, the luxuriant forests,
Subtle breeze, and—
Birds' songs.
Life is easy here, but fruitful.
I am calm, but heartily energetic.
Loving life comes from this tranquility.
But it can include the music of the birds.

3. Dr. Fisher s Studio Party

It is April.
Summer is coming.
In Dr. Fisher's house appear many people—
His piano students.

We gather,
and we talk about this semester.
We also talk about summer vacation.
The weather is beautiful.
And I feel Three colors are here.
Red—the sun,
Blue—the sky,
Green—the grassland.

Wow, the colors are simple but amazing.
And they seem to express the Professor's teaching.
Red—his passion and knowledge,
Blue—his inclusiveness and responsibility,
Green—his hospitality.

Lastly, his house is not in Athens, but very close.
Does that matter?

4. Summertime in Athens

"Summertime, and the living is easy…"
I have been loving this song…

I traveled with friends to New York City for Thanksgiving.
I was tired at night,
and I slept in a bed in a hotel in Manhattan.
I suddenly had an image of the summertime in Athens.
I felt so nostalgic.
By that time, I had experienced only one summer in Athens.

About the song by George Gershwin,
I hardly remembered the whole lyrics in my mind,
but only the first verse I know already immersed me
in the atmosphere—
the easy and beautiful summertime in Athens.

5. Busy Court Street

The city is small.
But Court Street is busy.
A dozen restaurants, one cinema, two barber shops, one bank, and one court.

I enjoy the deep-red bricks that cover the ground.
I enjoy the "one way" direction.
I also enjoy the crowd during weekends and big events.

I used to sit on a bench on Court Street,
experiencing how busy it is.
I felt calm and curious.

Years ago, the first time I walked on Court Street.
I felt, it was busy.
New York City should be like this,
because school life brought me a small world:
I just went to school and went back home every day.

My turning point was when I traveled to study abroad.
I studied at Ohio University in Athens.
From here, I started traveling around.

Now I just realized.
Athens is very small,
and Court Street is not busy.

I lived, I learned, and I loved.
I still feel Court Street is very busy.
Who cares?

6. Ohio University, the Beautiful

I rode my bicycle every morning—
Go down the hill.
I pushed my bike every night—
Go up the hill.
Of course, the city is very hilly,
and the university is very hilly,
without a doubt.

Every night, I arrived home,
I was so sweaty.
I was immersed in reading at night,
then I slept.
I still looked forward to riding down the hill to school next morning.
In here, forests and flowers—fragrance;
the river and the park—delicate;
the people—gentle and enthusiastic.

The beautifulness makes me feel never tired.
I climbed ups and downs with my bike.
But I am climbing to a bright future.
I am not finished—

Years later, every time, I went back to Ohio University,
I drove my car up the hill to the apartment where I lived.

I cannot remember how many times,
I drove my family and friends up to the place,

I found that the beautifulness is from the nature,
and from the spirit of the people.

Climbing up with a bicycle is very laborious.
Yet I never hate that—
Because,
my life here was blossoming…

7. Beautiful October

Time goes on and on.
Leaves started turning red and yellow.
The sky seems even higher and bluer.
The picturesque place is even more colorful.

The night is cooler.
But it is the harvest season.

I feel a little sad.
I wish the time could stop for a moment,
for the beautiful season,
for the charming scenery,
and for the youth to last.

Wait…how should I get sad?
I should enjoy my life here,
because there is no time to waste,
and no time to get sad.

Oh, no, the sadness means that I have enjoyed.

8. OU Boys and Girls

Many OU boys and girls helped me.
Vice versa—I helped them.

I feel healed when under pressure;
I feel strength when making progress…
But I do not feel sad when leaving OU,
because I still feel OU boys and girls are around me in my memory.

Don't just say they are great.

If, someday, I come across some of them in other places of the world.
I want to say "Hello."
And I want to tell them,
"I am one of the OU boys and girls."

9. Halloween Party in Athens

On Halloween night,
the crowd came to Court Street.
They dressed up,
in beautiful,
interesting,
or strange outfits.
They showed different characters.

The scene is quite hilarious.
We walked up and down on the not-very-long street.
They talked, laughed, and danced.

Oh, don't forget the food from the vendors.
The barbecue was delicious.
It is such an interesting time of chaos.
Life is like a showcase—
Wonderful,
Bizarre,
and Energetic.

10. Christmas Eve in Athens

Christmas Eve in Athens is strange.
Of course,
the strangeness came from the fact—
I hardly see people here.

Nobody? Anybody?

People are gone traveling,
or going back to their family.
No worries—
They will come back for spring semester.
We will reunite.

I enjoy the lonely city now.
I am not lonely—
I am just nostalgic—
For the past, the present, and the future.

My perspiration came from hard work in the past;
My calmness comes from rest in the present;
My hope will come from all the above in the future.

Oh, now the dinner is almost ready.
Our party is on—
We have somebody here, quite a few.
But we feel happy.

11. Christmas Day in Athens

Oh, Christmas Day—
I was thrilled!
Early in the morning,
I got up and walked to school.
It was a cloudy day,
but not very cold.
Why did not I feel any festive atmosphere?
I tried to seek that.

I studied at school until about noon.
Then, I walked back home for lunch.
During the walk,
I failed to find the holiday condition—
Everywhere was closed,
and I saw nobody.

Finally, you could not imagine,
that I still had a wonderful Christmas.
I phoned several friends.
We collected some stuff.
We made dumplings.
We chatted and laughed.
Wonderful life is not from outside conditions,
but from our hearts and efforts.

12. Going back to Ohio University

From where do I go back to OU?
From different places.

I cannot remember how many times
I took a bus to return.
But I always think of the first day and the first night—
I arrived in Athens.
That was many years ago.

It was so hard—I was a stranger.
I also think twenty years later or fifty years later.
At those times,
I will go back to OU.
I could also be a stranger, again.
Even though I am not a stranger right now…

It does not matter for this question.
No matter whether this place recognizes me,
I have this place in my heart.
No matter how much I travel in the world,
I am rooted in here.
No matter how time flies,
I will have the same love.

Why could I be a stranger?
The answer is:
People do not know me.
And I do not know people here.
That is destiny.

Wait…

If there is destiny,
I was never and will never be a stranger.
I will still make efforts to create my career in my life,
Like from my first day here.
I will make a living, and seek to live well,
Like from my first day here.

I do belong here,
And,
It does matter.

1. The Unforgettable Energy of Spring
(Waltz)

24
30
dim.
mp
cresc.
35
40
mp
dim.
45
cresc.
f

rall.
a tempo
mf
mp

76
82
cresc.
88
mf
94
dim.
100
f

105
111
116
121
126

133
mp
cresc.
139
sf
145
rall.
f
dim.
Tempo I
151
mp
157

163
cresc.
169
175
dim.
181
mp
cresc.
mf
186
f

191
ff
196
202
208
sempre f
214

219
225
rall.
dim.
231
dim.
Adagio Tranquillo
p
236
242
cresc.

249
mf
dim.
254
p
259
pp
p dim. smorzando
263
rall.
pp

2. The Nighttime of Athens

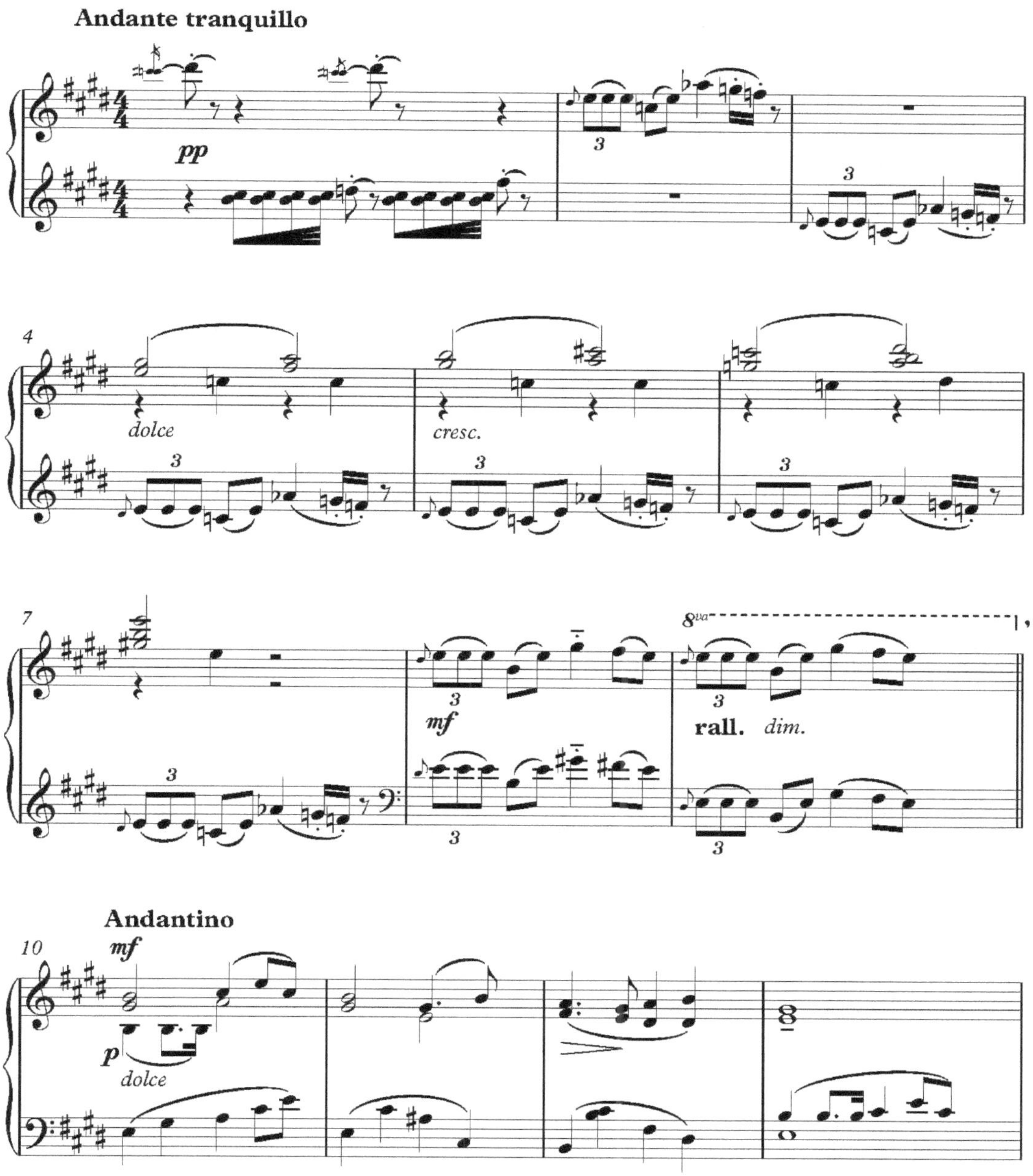

Andante tranquillo

pp

dolce

cresc.

mf

rall. *dim.*

Andantino

mf

p *dolce*

14
18
22
26
molto rit..
30
A tempo
mf
3
3
espress.
3
3

accel.
Più mosso
mf
f
cresc.
ff
smorzando
molto rit.
p
Tempo primo
mp
pp

50
ff
55
mf
pp
59
63
5
5
8vb
ad lib.
mf
66
espress.
3

69
3
3
8vb
8va
3
mf
3
mp
73
3
3
75
p
76
8va
3
3
pp
rall.
smorzando
3
3

››

3. Dr. Fisher's Studio Party
(Prelude, Toccata, and Fugue)

Prelude
Adagio

13
rit.
dim.
Toccata
Allegretto
17
mf
21
p
mf
sub p
cresc.
25
mf cresc.
29
cresc.

33
f
dim.
37
p
cresc.
41
ff
44
47
p

51
56
pp
cresc.
61
non-legato
64
rit.
non-legato
dim.
rit.
Fugue
67
Andante
mp
legato
sempre legato

71
non-legato
74
cresc.
77
80
83
f
f
3
cresc.
3

86
3
3
3
3
ff

4. Summertime in Athens
(Fantasy)

13
17
dim.
20
21
cresc.
23
f
26

29
dim.
32
mf
35
f
rit.
39
Più mosso
pp misterioso
41

43
2
45
47
cresc.
49
dim.
4
4
ppp
51
similie

53
54
55
mf
cresc.
57
molto cresc.
59
ff
Meno mosso
p
expressivo

62
rit.
Andante Tranquillo
pp
66
69
rit.
a tempo
71
dim.
73
rit.
ppp

5. Busy Court Street

17
20
mp
cresc.
23
26
8va
f
sempre f
30
8va
mf
p cresc.

34
mp
37
cresc.
40
43
46

49
cresc.

52
rall.
dim.

55
Andante
p dolce

59

rall.
a tempo
63
pp
cresc.
mf
67
71
75
rit.
dim.
pp

78
pp
accel.
cresc.

Tempo primo
81
f

85
accel.
sub p
cresc.
3
3

88
a tempo
ff
3
3
3
3

6. Ohio University, the Beautiful

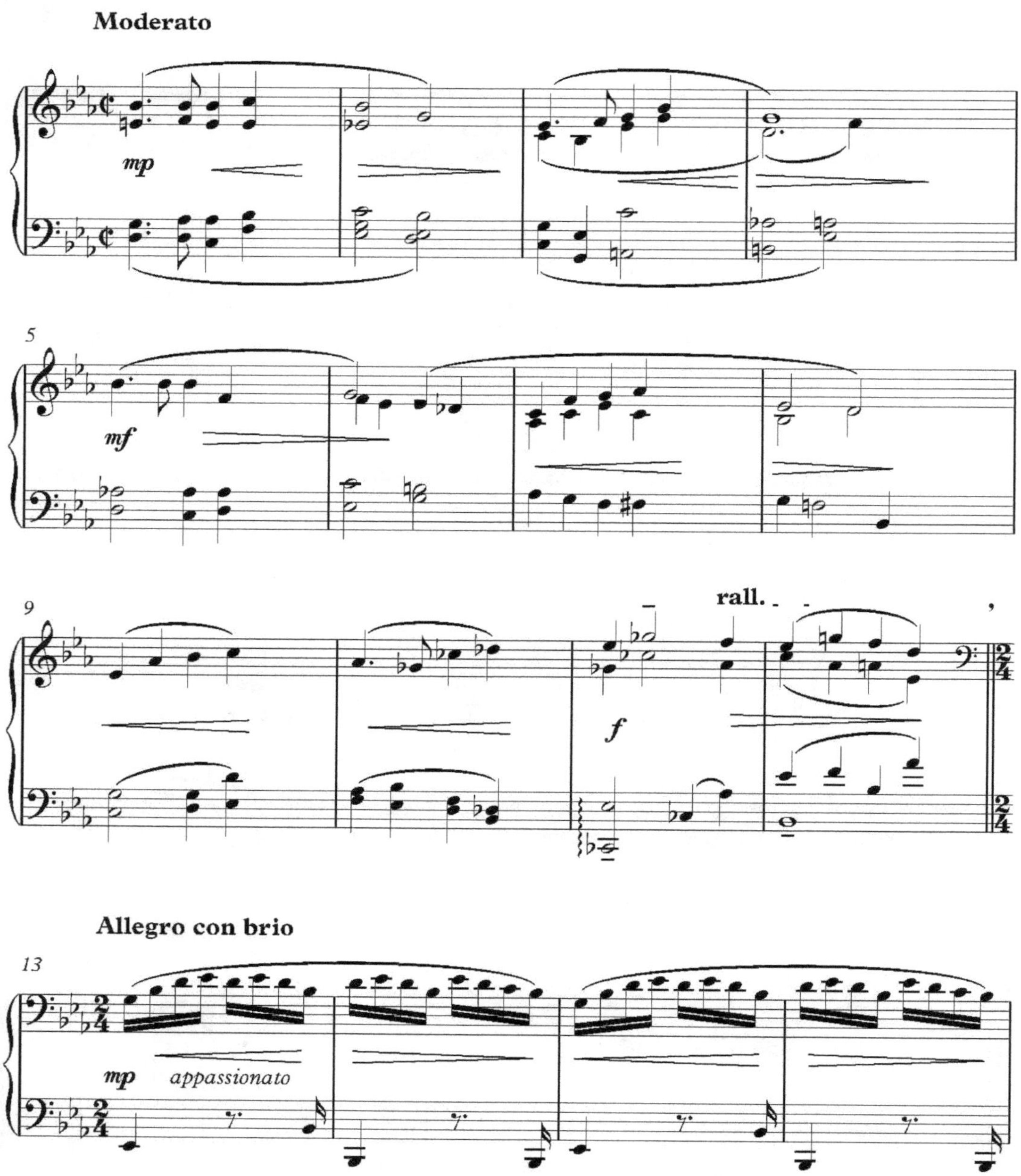

Moderato

mp

5

mf

9

rall.

f

Allegro con brio

13

mp *appassionato*

17
mf
simile
p
21
mf
p
25
cresc.
f
29
sub p
33
cresc.

37
3
3
3
3
3
3
f
cresc.
41
3
3
ff
sf
45
sf
49
sf
53
rit.
pesante
dim.

57
Adagio
dolce
p
61
mp
65
p
mf
ad lib.
69
rit.
dim.
A tempo
pp
dolce
mp
73

77
5
5
5
5
3
3
3
3

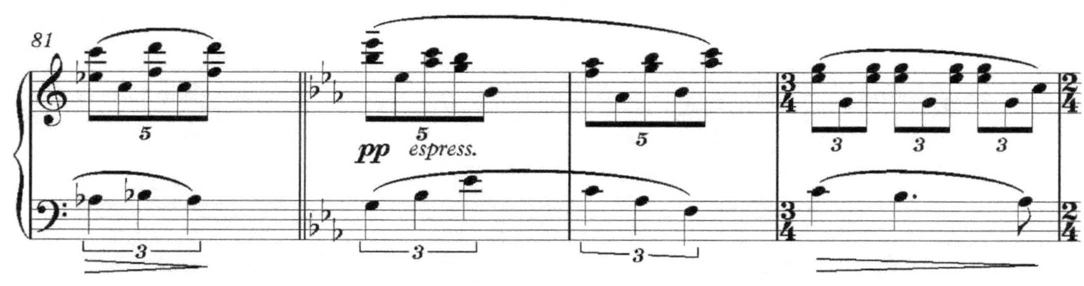
81
5
5
5
3
3
3
3
pp *espress.*
3
3

85
3
3
3
3
3
3
tr
tr
pp accel.
3
3

89
8va
misterioso

Allegro con brio
93
mp
97
f
p
101
p
cresc.
f
105
sf
sf
sf
109
ff
sf

113
117
sub. mp
cresc.
121
f
cresc.
8va
ff
sf
125
sempre ff
129
ff

7. Beautiful Octorber
(Barcarolle)

17
mf
p
cresc.
21
f
p
f
rit.
p
25
a tempo
p
29
mf
33
f
p

37
cresc.
41
2
2
2
2
f
45
ff
49
52
Più mosso
mp

56
60
mf
64
ff
mf
cresc.
67
f
cresc.

71
ff

rall.
Tempo I
75
8va
dim.
p

79
mf

83
mp

86
pp
dolcissimo
89
92
pp
95
rall..
4
4
a tempo
mf

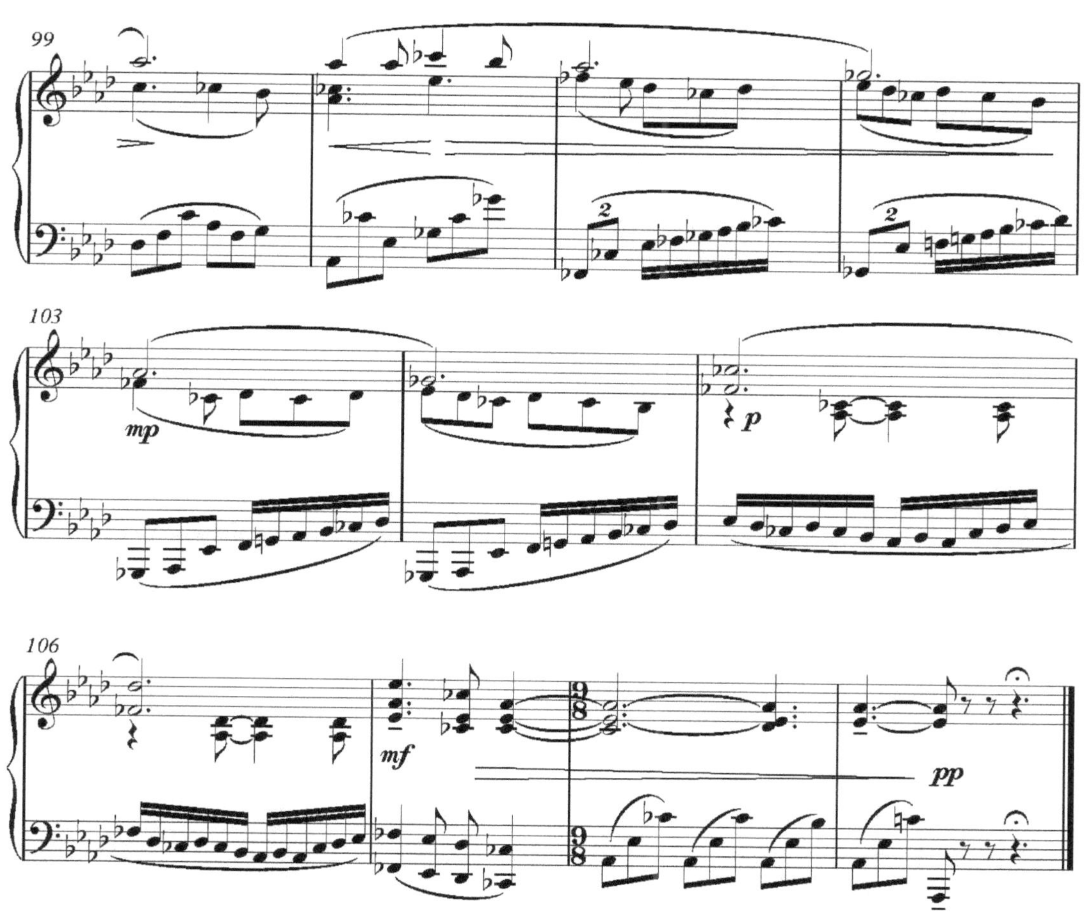
99
mp
103
p
106
mf
pp

8. OU Boys and Girls
(Tarantella)

17
simile
21
cresc.
25
29
f
cresc.
33
f
sub p

37
cresc.
f
sub p
41
rall.
Meno mosso
45
mf
49
53
p
cresc.

57
61
f
leggiero
65
dim.
70
p
74
cresc.

77
ff
80
dim.
83
rall. .
Tempo primo
p
staccato
86
90

94
mf
98
similie
f
102
mp
cresc.
106
f
mf

110
cresc.
mf
cresc.
f
115
cresc.
ff
sf
sf
sf
sf
sf
sf

9. Halloween Party in Athens
(March)

14
f
marcato
17
sub mp
20
molto cresc.
23
f
26
cresc.

29
ff

31
8va
sempre ff
8vb
f dolce

34

37
rall.
a tempo
mp leggiero
f
rit.

Tempo primo
41
p leggiero
staccato
44
cresc.
f
marcato
47
sub mp
50
53
ff
pp leggiero

56
59
cresc.
61
f
leggiero
dim.
64
rall.
67
Lento
p
dolce
5
3
Tempo primo
ff
3
3
8vb

10. Christmas Eve in Athens
(Prelude and Polka)

mf
rall.
Lento
mf
legato

27
cresc.
31
f
34
mf
dim.
38
mp
p
rall.

Polka
Allegretto
44
mf
49
p
53
f
8vb
57
mp
61
p
cresc.

65
f
p
69
cresc.
73
f
cresc.
rall.
a tempo
77
ff
ad lib.
12
8vb
81
ad lib.
12
accel.
sempre ff
8vb

84
88
dim.
f
92
Lento
sempre f
dim.
3
95
dim.
Andante Sostenuto
99
p
pp
6

104
8va
Presto
f
cresc.
ff
6

11. Christmas Day in Athens
(Nocturn)

rall.
Più mosso
mf
mp
poco a poco cresc.
mf
mp
poco a poco cresc.

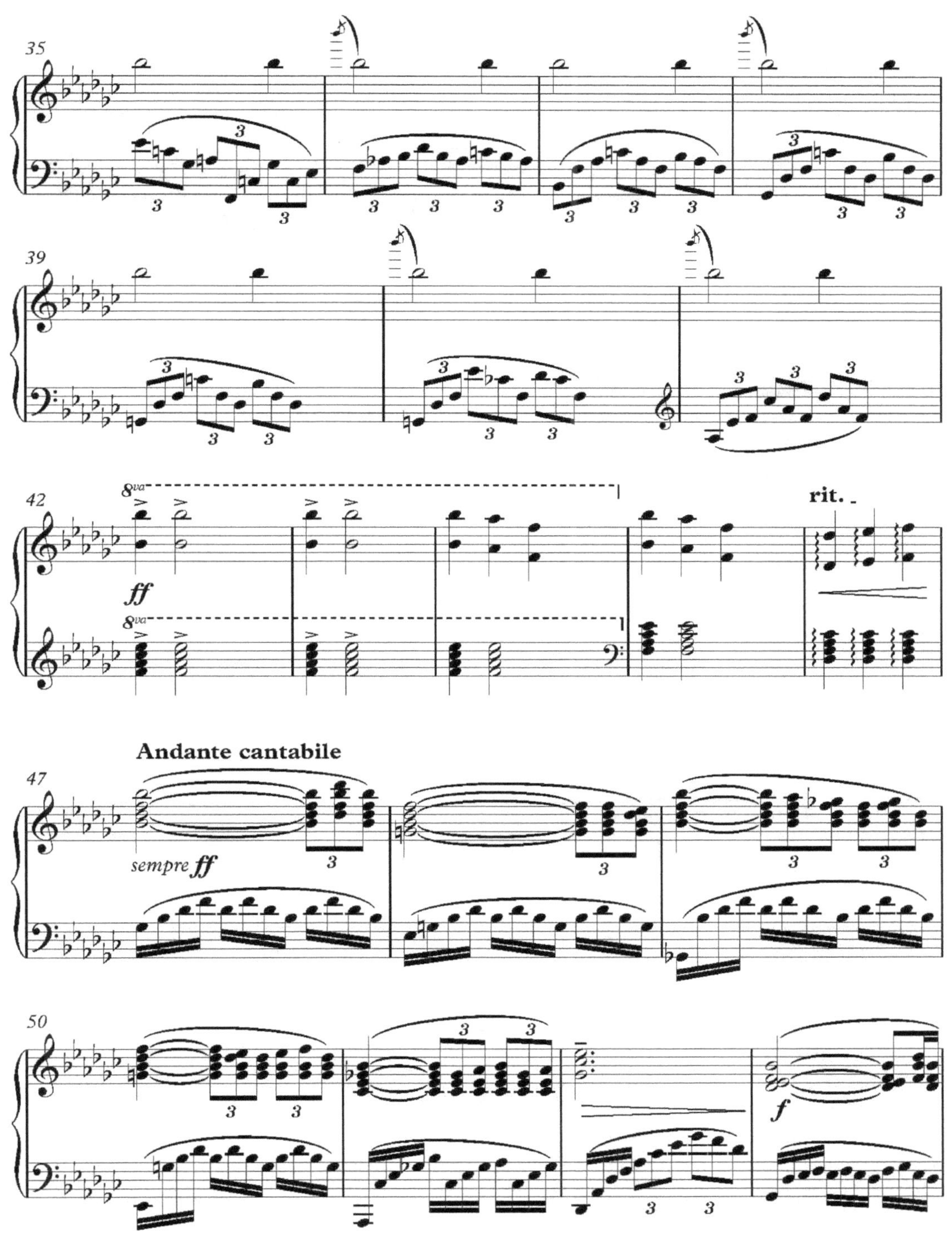
35
39
42
8va
ff
rit.
Andante cantabile
47
sempre ff
50
f

54
cresc.
57
f solemn
ad lib.
63
rall.
Lento
mf
69
72
8vb

12. Going Back to Ohio University
(Tango)

20
dim.
24
cresc.
ff
p
27
30
f
p
33

36
6
40
rit.
Più mosso
mp
44
48
poco rit.
p
dolce
pp
a tempo
52
poco accel.
mf

56
3
mf
60
3
f
sub p
64
Allegro
ff
cadenza
l.h.
r.h.
simile
69
ff

73
Allegretto ♪.=132
mf
77
poco rall.
a tempo
cresc.
80
poco rit.
83
mf a tempo
mp
86
molto cresc.

poco rit.
f
a tempo
p
molto rit.
ad lib.
mf
a tempo
p
dim. smorzando
molto rit.
sf
ff
sf

CPSIA information can be obtained
at www.ICGtesting.com
Printed in the USA
LVHW060038270321
682643LV00003B/72

9 781648 045769